Kathy Costanzo holds a bachelor's degree in music education and a master's degree in elementary education. She often incorporates music into other academic subjects in her classroom. Crafting educational materials and manipulatives with a glue gun is a common sight. Married with three children who have been inspirations to her work in their own ways, Kathy resides in a quaint town on Lake Ontario. She enjoys combing the beach for treasured keepsakes. Her classroom reflects her passions – infusing learning with creativity, finding teachable moments in everyday interests, and treasuring family connections along life's journey.

Kathy Costanzo

CAN WE SING IT AGAIN?

AUSTIN MACAULEY PUBLISHERS™

LONDON • CAMBRIDGE • NEW YORK • SHARJAH

Ordering Information
Quantity sales: Special discounts are available on quantity purchases by corporations, associations, and others. For details, contact the publisher at the address below.

Publisher's Cataloging-in-Publication data
Costanzo, Kathy
Can We Sing It Again?

ISBN 9798889104339 (Paperback)
ISBN 9798889104346 (ePub e-book)

Library of Congress Control Number: 2023918271

www.austinmacauley.com/us

First Published 2024
Austin Macauley Publishers LLC
40 Wall Street, 33rd Floor, Suite 3302
New York, NY 10005
USA

mail-usa@austinmacauley.com
+1 (646) 5125767

I would like to thank Constance MacKay, Randy Andropolis, David Tower, and my incredible family. You never know what effect you have on others and I am grateful for your influence.

Five Little Pumpkins

Nursery Rhyme

It has been said…

- that pumpkin is a fruit, not a vegetable.
- pumpkin pie was not served at the first Thanksgiving.

- that October 26th is unofficially National Pumpkin Day.

Five Little Pumpkins
(subtraction)

1. Have the children seated on the floor. Display the visual of the gate. Show the class how the pumpkins stick on the gate. Hide the gate and take one pumpkin off. Show the children the gate again and ask if they can tell what happened. They will say that you took one pumpkin off. Praise the children and do that activity again.
2. Take off however many pumpkins you like. The children have to tell you how many you took off. They can add up to five, but see if your children can subtract. "I had five pumpkins and I took two off. Five minus one and minus one more equals…?"
- Extension idea: Use Velcro or make your own felt board. Felt will stick to felt. If you are using paper pumpkins, then laminate the pumpkins and affix the scratchy portion of the Velcro to the back of the pumpkin. This part of the Velcro will stick nicely to felt.

Five Little Snakes

(subtraction)

Five little snakes said, "Look at me, I'm swimming under logs and around a tall tree." Then along came an alligator, slow as can be… and SNAP!

1. This poem is based on the poem "Five Little Monkeys." I do not have an instrument that sounds like monkeys, but instead think maracas, or even a rain stick, to resemble the sound of a rattlesnake. In other words, the words have been changed from the original speech piece in order to have the instruments sound like the characters.

2. The class sits on the floor in a circle with the five snakes on the floor spread out in front of you. Say the poem rhythmically and with expression to make the story interesting. Clap loudly on the word "SNAP" and take away one snake. Say the poem again but this time change the words to say four snakes.

3. Invite the children to join you in saying the rest of the poem until you get to the last "SNAP." The children clap on the "SNAP" words. When all of

the snakes are gone, say, "All gone," using a toothy grin while you smack your lips and rub your tummy.

4. Ask the students which character says, "All gone." They will tell you that is the snake part. Practice this part together. Show the guiro. I like to use the crow sounder instead, which is like a tone block and a guiro combined. Scrape the crow sounder (guiro) very slowly with the stick part of the mallet. You say the alligator part slowly and quietly, so scrape the instrument slowly. You want to mimic the sound of the alligator creeping. Be sure to ask the children why you are saying the poem slowly and quietly. When you say "SNAP" loudly, all hit their instruments loudly with their mallet on that word. Pass these instruments out to half of the class and practice until everyone plays together on the word "SNAP!"

5. Show the class a maraca. Shake the maraca and then compare the rattle sound to the tail of a rattle snake. Since the maraca is supposed to play the part of the snake talking, only play on the part that reads "Look at me, I'm swimming under logs and around a tall tree." Shake on the snake's talking part. Again, say the poem rhythmically and with expression. Give the maracas to the rest of the class.

6. Put the whole poem together, reminding the class that the instruments never play together at the same time.

7. Switch instruments and perform the poem again. This way each child will get to play both

instruments. I like to have only half of the group play instruments and have the other half recite the poem. Some children find it difficult to speak and play an instrument at the same time.

- Extension idea: Talk about the snakes on the floor. They are a visual/manipulative for subtracting one from a number. Write an equation on the board, 5–1 for example. Do a couple of subtraction examples together, make sure to only subtract one from each number, Can the class say the poem in its entirety without the snakes for a visual?
- Extension idea: Make your own maracas and rain sticks!
- Vocabulary: rain stick, maraca, creeping, soft, loud.

Five Red Apples

(subtraction)

Kathy Costanzo

1. Put five red apples on the felt apple tree. The apples have a strip of Velcro on the back so the apples stay hung upon the tree. Have five children stand in a line next to the tree, these children are the apple pickers and can dance while everyone sings. When you sing the part about Farmer Dave, the first child picks an apple off of the tree and takes a nice LOUD pretend bite out of the apple (my students think the eating loudly and "gobbling of the apple" part is the best sound effect!). Put the apple down. Finish the song with the next child picking off the next apple as you sing about four, then three, then eventually no red apples on the tree.

Five Red Apples

Kathy Costanzo

Flower Song

(High and low voices)

1. The children will hold a flower of some kind as they are squatting down and singing. As each note gets higher the children's bodies get a little higher (to match the music). At the end of the song, the children are standing upright.
2. On the "Grow up!" low to high part at the very end the children squat down and then quickly stand up, in order for their bodies to match the pitches in the music.

- Extension ideas: Change the words to a tree growing.
- Hold pictures of flowers that the children colored.

FLOWER SONG

Kathy Costanzo

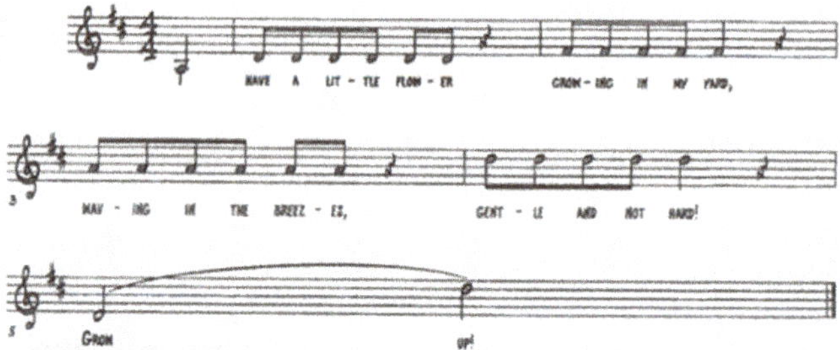

Hokey Pokey

Traditional

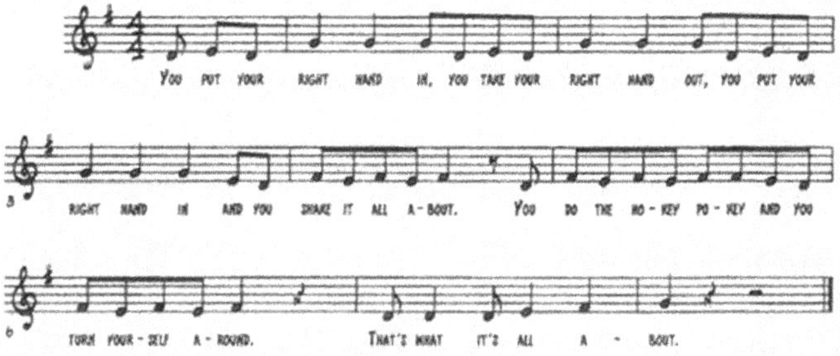

It has been said…

- that Jimmy Kennedy, an Irish songwriter, created a dance in 1942 that included an instructional song to go with it. He called it 'The Hokey Cokey."
- Robert Degan and Joe Brier, two Pennsylvania musicians, recorded "The Hokey Pokey Dance" in 1946. It was used to entertain summer vacationers at the Pocono Mountains resorts.

Hokey Pokey
(Colors and shapes)

1. Cut out four shapes (circle, square, rectangle, and triangle) out of four vibrant colors. Put these shapes in a regular white business envelope but DO NOT SEAL the envelope. Children are seated in a circle. When you pass out a filled envelope to each child, really hype up the fact that they are all getting a piece of mail and DO NOT OPEN the envelope yet. No peeking! The anticipation makes the children so excited to see what is inside.

2. When all have an envelope and you are seated, instruct the children to carefully open the envelope flap and take out the items inside. Add a couple "oohs" and "aahhs" to add to the excitement.

3. Each child has four different shapes and four different colors in their envelope and they are to spread these items out on the floor in front of them. Begin to sing the song Hokey Pokey but change the words to "put your circle in, take your circle out" or "put your blue shape in, take your blue shape out." Do the rest of the song with the dance like usual.

4. When the game is finished and everyone is putting their pieces back into the envelope, make sure the children DO NOT lick the envelope to seal it.

Horses

(counting)

1. Sit on the floor with the children while holding the barn and singing the song. Pass out a few of the horses. The children that are holding the horses put their horse through the slit in the back of the barn (sometimes two children and sometimes five, etc.). Placing the horse through the slit in the barn is a fine-motor activity. At the end of the song have a child lift the barn so everyone can count the number of horses that were placed inside while singing.

2. Show the class a drum and explain how you want it held as well as how you want it played. Hit the drum to match how many horses that were counted. One drum beat if there is one horse, five drum beats if there were five horses, etc., Pass the drum around the circle for all to get a turn to play the count of how many horses there were placed inside the barn.

- Extension idea: Make your own drums out of a can that comes with a plastic lid (coffee or oatmeal for example). Cover the base with paper and color the paper so the students can personalize their own drums.

HORSES

Kathy Costanzo

It has been said…

- that horses have the largest eyes of any land mammal.
- that horse's teeth take up more space in their head than their brain.
- that horses can sleep both lying down and standing up.

I'm a Frog!

(High and low voices)

1. Children are holding a frog of some kind as they are squatting down. As each note gets higher, the children's bodies get a little higher (to match the music). The children can use their super low voices for the "ribbit" sound effect.

2. You can also change it up a bit…
Hop up high (high voice with frogs held high), hop down low (voices and frogs down low), hop really fast, hop really slow (moving their bodies and frogs appropriately).

- Extension idea: Talk of rhyming words and vocabulary words (fast, slow, high, low voices for example),

- Make sure children do not confuse a quiet voice with a low voice. Those terms get confused easily.

I'M A FROG!

Kathy Costanzo

I'm a Turkey

Traditional French Tune

Lyrics by Kathy Costanzo

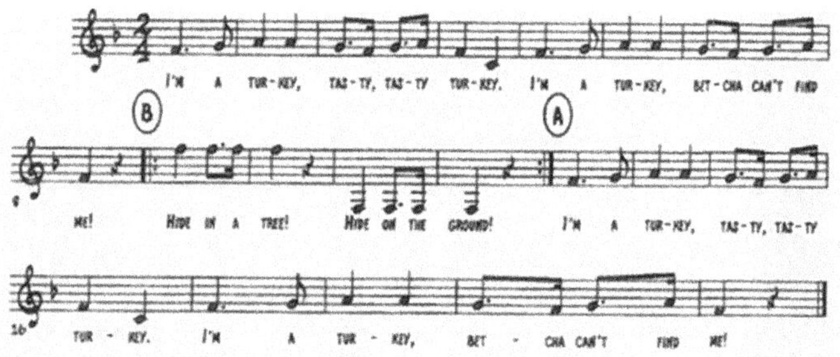

It has been said…

1. that Benjamin Franklin thought the turkey would have been a better national symbol than the bald eagle,
2. that yes, indeed, turkeys are not a flightless bird!

I'm a Turkey
(High and low voices)

1. Teach the A section and sing together a few times.
2. Teach the B section. Ask the children if they notice what your voice is doing. Guide the students into describing that you are using your high and low voices. They demonstrate their voices changing from high to low and use their bodies (tippy toes and squatting, hands held up high and down low). Repeat the B section three times.
3. Sing the song in its ABA pattern. Discuss the ABA pattern and write it on the board.
4. Pass out the turkey manipulatives. (Go to a craft store and purchase one-and-one-half inch high felt turkeys used for scrapbooking or other crafts. Use sturdy tape to attach the shapes to popsicle sticks). During the A section the students walk like turkeys while singing and holding their turkey sticks. During the B section they freeze their feet where they are but go from tippy toes to squatting low to match their singing voices and the lyrics. Really have them concentrate on changing their voices to match their body position of high and low.
5. Choose a child to be a "cook." This child stands in the middle of the room. At the end of the song, the cook taps a child who used his/her high and low voices correctly. This child becomes the new cook. The cook is to listen intently on voice changes.
- Extension ideas: Use whatever manipulatives you can find that you could move from high to low

(maybe felt birds or artificial birds from a craft store).

- Change the lyrics to match different manipulatives and/or seasons.

Itsy Bitsy Spider

Traditional

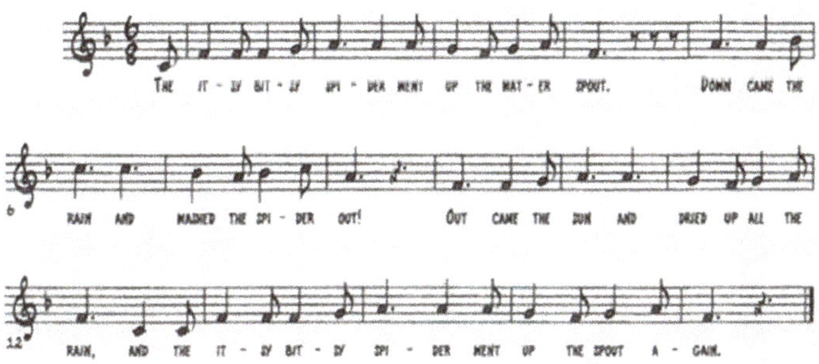

Itsy Bitsy Spider
(Dramatization and sound effects)

1. Sing the song with the children, making sure everyone is familiar with the song.
2. Buy or make a large spider. Many dollar stores have inexpensive, colorful yet hairy spiders for decorations in the fall. Tie some fishing line around the spider's neck. Put a little loop in the other end of the fishing line. Hang the spider over something and pull on the line, your spider should look like it is crawling upwards.
3. Make a large sunshine from yellow construction paper and a dowel rod or yard stick. Tape the sunshine to the rod.
4. Play cymbals and a rain stick.
5. Match the lyrics to the activity.
6. Children switch instruments and props.

- Extension idea: Make your own rain stick and cymbals.

Lyrics	**Activity**
The itsy-bitsy spider went up the water spout	Pull up the spider like it is climbing
Down came the rain and	Play the rain stick
Washed the spider out	Play the cymbals while you allow the spider to quickly go back down. Do not allow the child holding the string to let go.
Out came the sun and dried up all the rain	A child holds up the sunshine
And the itsy-bitsy spider went up the spout again	Pull up the spider again

It has been said…

- that spiders can survive in outer space.
- that spiders live on every continent, except for Antarctica.
- that when a spider is done with its web, it will eat the spun silk in order to restock its supply for the next web.

I Wish I Were a Fish

(High and low voices)

1. During the A section, the children hold fish puppets while they tiptoe around the room singing.
2. During the B section, the children stay in place and move their fish puppets to match the music. Fishes held high on high notes, then arc down and bend knees to use low voices on the low notes while the fish puppet is "swimming' down low. Repeat the B section two or three times, then go back to the beginning and tiptoe again.

I Wish I Was a Fish

Kathy Costanzo

Mary Wore Her Red Dress

American Folk Song

2. Mary wore her red hat
3. Mary wore her red shoes
4. Mary wore her red gloves
5. Mary looked so lovely…

It has been said…

- that red does not make bulls angry.
- that red is the first color a baby sees.

Mary Wore Her Red Dress
(Shapes, like a puzzle)

1. Make a felt board of a girl with a face and hair. I do not add a bellybutton. My students will often say that the girl is naked. I then tell them that she is wearing a leotard, which is sort of like a bathing suit. I point out that if she was naked, we would see her belly button, so therefore she is definitely wearing something. They never ask again.

2. Hand the clothing pieces out to some of the children. There are not enough pieces for all so the children are reminded of how to share. When you sing about wearing a red dress, a child puts the dress on Mary. Same with the hat and shoes. I like Mary to be giving us all the "thumbs up" sign and this is where it gets tricky for some children The children need to make sure the shoes are on the correct feet as well as the gloves with the thumbs facing up. The traditional lyrics say that Mary is a red bird for the last verse, I just changed the words to say that Mary looks so lovely.

3. Take all of the pieces off and quickly review what the words are.

4. Sing again, this time all the children will sing with you. Give the clothing pieces to different children so that everyone will get a turn.

- Extension idea: Make another outfit for Mary that is all green or blue or yellow. You can mix up the outfits for a red dress, yellow hat, blue shoes and green gloves if you want to get psychedelic with her outfit!

Old MacDonald

Traditional

Old MacDonald
(Dramatization)

1. Teach the song to the students. Add any animal that might be on a farm and use the glove as a visual for an aid in remembering the items and order.

2. Use a regular white glove and glue a piece of Velcro to each fingertip. Use foam pieces and glue the other portion of the Velcro to the back of each foam piece so that the pieces will stick to the glove fingertips.

3. Remember that this song lends itself to changing the words and word order, nothing is written in stone.

- Extension ideas: Maybe Old MacDonald had a Zoo. Or Mrs. Johnson had a class (and cut out the

children's pictures and put Velcro on the back so
the kids will be stuck to the glove).

Use the glove for other songs that have five characters,
such as:
"Five Little Monkeys", "Five Little Pumpkins" or
"Five Little Speckled Frogs"

Red and Yellow and Blue

Kathy Costanzo

Red and Yellow and Blue
(colors)

1. Read a book about colors to the children. I use "Monsters Love Colors" by Mike Austin, "Little Green Peas" by Keith Baker, or "Swatch, The Girl Who Loved Color" by Julia Denos. You can use any color book that you like.

2. Talk to the children about the primary colors. Those colors are used to make all other colors.

3. Sing the song Red and Yellow and Blue to the children and invite them to sing along with you.

4. Make streamers for the children to wave while they are singing. Give two streamers of the same color to each child, one for each hand. The red streamers make zig zag patterns down low (flower height). The yellow streamers circle over their heads (high

like the sun). The blue streamers swirl like figure eights close to the floor (like water on the ground). Do your streamer motion when the color of your streamer is sung. Make sure the children use big arm motions so the streamers will be seen moving beautifully!

- Extension ideas: Streamers can be made of thin ribbon, just use many taped to a tongue depressor or popsicle stick.

Streamers can be made of thicker ribbon or silky fabric. Tie a loop at one end so the children can hold the fabric with no stick.

Streamers can actually be scarves. Scarves look pretty floating around the room.

- Use colored cellophane papers to demonstrate how to mix colors to create new ones.
- Layer the sheets of cellophane.
- Colored water works well to mix.

It has been said…

- that blue was once seen as a color for the working class during ancient times. The wealthy wore white, red and black.
- that pink is a relaxing color.
- that Isaac Newton found that light influences color.

- that white was considered the safest color. White vehicles were less likely to be involved in automobile accidents resulting in death.

See the Little Fishy

(High and low voices)

1. Children sing while holding fish puppets. Fish are held high when voices sing high. Hold fish low when the music is low.

SEE THE LITTLE FISHY

Kathy Costanzo

Shake Them Bones

Kathy Costanzo

Verse 2 Legs can bend so you can run and jump, run and jump, run and jump. Legs can bend so you can run and jump. Legs connect to your foot.

Verse 3 Arms and shoulders shake and hug, shake and hug, shake and hug. Arms and shoulders shake and hug. Arms connect to your hands.

Verse 4 Your heads contains your brain and your eyes and ears, eyes and ears, eyes and ears. Your head contains your brain and your eyes and ears. Your head sits on your neck.

Shake Them Bones
(Body parts)

1. Purchase an inexpensive, plastic, two-foot-long segmented skeleton. These are readily available during the fall. Cut the skeleton in six pieces where it is segmented connecting to the torso. In other words, separate the head, torso, and then each individual limb. Be sure to keep the feet and hands attached to the limbs.

2. Glue the torso to the middle of a two-and-one-half foot piece of felt, I prefer black felt for this activity. Hang this skeleton visual just high enough for the children to be able to reach the neck.

3. Glue a generous piece of Velcro to the back of the skull. Use the hooked pieces, they adhere nicely to felt. Glue more hooked pieces of Velcro to the back of each upper arm at the shoulder area and more Velcro at the top of the leg bones where they used to be connected at the pelvis. Your skull, arms and

leg pieces can now be easily put on and taken off of the fabric.

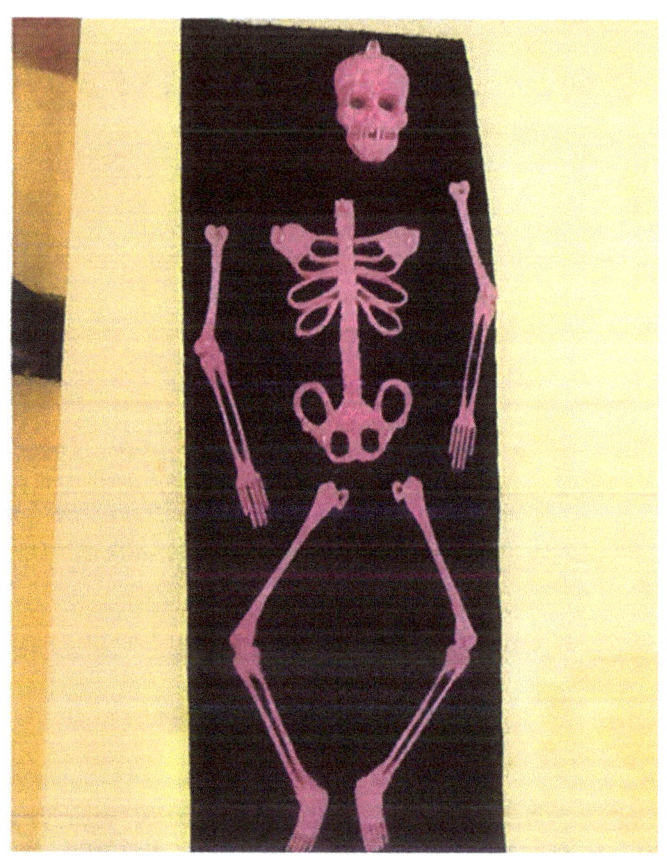

Sing About Peace

Kathy Costanzo

Verse 1 – Country

Verse 2 – Family

Verse 3 – Classroom

Sing About Peace
(Getting along)

1. Teach the A section to your students. Make sure all children do the cut-off together after four beats on the word 'peace." If they do not cut-off together then the song will sound sloppy.

2. The A section has three clave (rhythm stick) taps to play after the word "peace." First have the students clap where the clave taps occur, then give some children claves to play. I usually give a pair of rhythm sticks to each child so everyone can play. When I use this song at a performance, I assign claves to just a few children.

3. Teach the B section to your students. There are three verses (country, family, classroom). My students sit on the floor in a circle with their legs crossed in front of them. When your legs are crossed you create what I call a "bowl" with your legs. Instruct your students to put the sticks in the "bowl" that their legs make. Have your students hold hands with the child next to them and gently sway side to side. You want the sticks to be close by, yet easy to stash quietly or pick up quickly, so the bowl works nicely. For verse one we hold hands, verse two is when we link elbows (you will actually have to teach what that is), and on verse three wrap your arms around the shoulders of the person next to you. There is a short fermata at the end of each section. This is just long enough to pick

up sticks or put away the sticks quickly into the leg bowls.

4. The form of the song is ABA. Please allow the students to figure that out, with your assistance.

Please take the time to really stress how everyone in our world needs to get along and cooperate with one another. We need to get along in the classroom, at home, in our community, and globally.

It has been said…

- that Nelson Mandela said, "If you want to make peace with your enemy, you have to work with your enemy. Then he becomes your partner."

Teddy Bear

Folk Song

It has been said…

- that September 9th is national Teddy Bear Day.
- that the teddy bear got its name from a story about Teddy Roosevelt. In 1902 Roosevelt refused to shoot a bear cub while on a hunting trip.

Teddy Bear
(Dramatic play)

1. Instruct the children to listen to the entire song. Someone in the song is going to be giving directions. When the song is over, the children have to raise their hands and tell you what directions were given. Who were those directions given to? Sing the song to the children. Hopefully, they can tell you the correct answers,

2. Teach the song one phrase at a time. After four phrases put the pieces together. When you sing the other four phrases put those pieces together. Eventually, put the whole song together and sing it in its entirety.

3. Have the children stand and act out the motions sung in the song.

4. Each child will need a teddy bear. It can be a real teddy bear or one that you've made from paper. If you use paper bears, make sure they are laminated for strength. Instruct the children to be careful with these bears because they are made of paper and paper is easy to rip.

5. Use the teddy bears as a prop to dramatize the story. At the end, all bears should be on the floor and children should have their hands together under one cheek pretending to be asleep. Have the children peek with one eye open to see if they did the game properly.

Ten Little Indians

Traditional

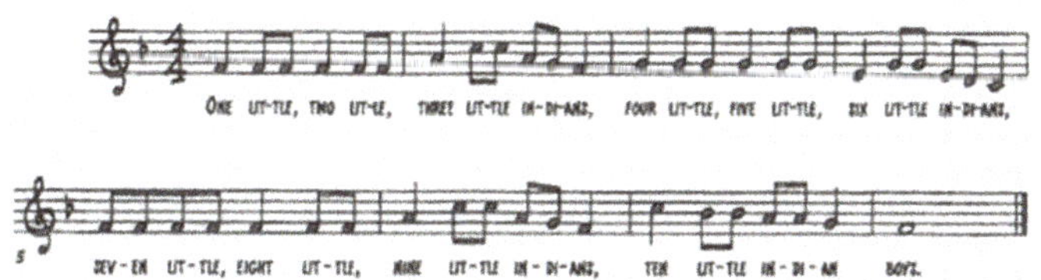

Ten Little Indians
(Recognizing numbers)

1. Teach the song Ten Little Indians to the children. Change the words depending on the prop that you are using. In the fall I use candy corn or jack-o-lanterns and in the winter, I use candy canes. Make 10 of these cards with the picture that you are using on the front. Number each card 1-10. This game is an aid to help children recognize numbers.

2. The number is written on the card with a visual of what that number is. The candy cane, for example, has 10 stripes on the 10 card and six stripes on the six card and etc. The same goes for the candy corn cards. If you cannot add the number of stripes to match the number on the card, then put the matching number of dots on the card. If a child does not recognize the number, they can count the stripes or dots.

3. Decorative napkins are perfect for this activity. You can have any picture/napkin that you want on the front of the card depending on what unit you are studying. Tape the napkin to a heavy piece of an oak tag to make it sturdier, add the numbers with the corresponding dots to the front, and presto! Easy visuals! Laminate whenever you can.

It has been said…

*   that "Ten Little Indians" is an old nursery rhyme from 1868. The original song was composed in the

USA by Septimus Winner. The song had 10 verses and was called 'Ten Little Injuns."

- that the song 'Ten Little Indians" is a great song for teaching counting.

Brown Bear, Brown Bear, What Do You See?

Kathy Costanzo

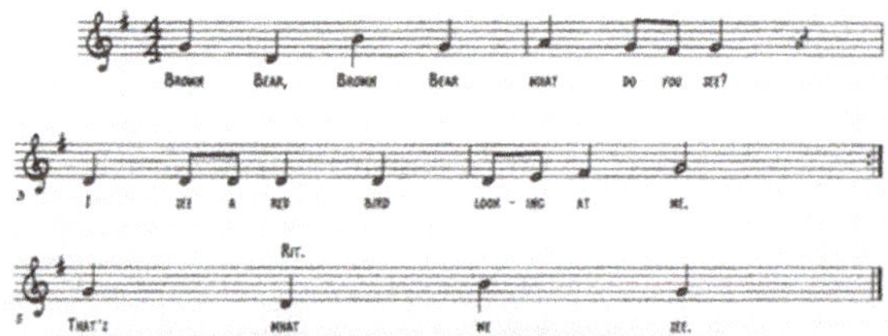

Brown Bear, Brown Bear, What Do You See?
(Dramatization, colors)

1. Sing, not just read, the book by Bill Martin Jr. and Eric Carle. The text is singsong and repetitive, perfect for little children. By the time you sing about the third animal, the children will know how the song goes. Sing it again and invite the children to sing the entire story with you.

2. Make puppets! I use various colors of felt and a glue gun. You can decorate your puppets with feathers, fur, sequins, yarn, buttons, netting or anything else you can think of to make your puppets look like the story characters. Make two or three of each character so that each child can hold a puppet for the story dramatization. use various shades of brown for the bear puppets and different shades for the blue horses, etc. Teach/review the concept of light and dark colors. Create only animal puppets. The children are the children in the story. Do not make a teacher puppet, allow that part be yours!

3. The children are sitting in a circle, in order for everyone to see each other. Hand out the puppets in order of the story going around the circle. The children on the left are the brown bears, and keep going around the circle until the children on your very right are the goldfish.

4. Hold up the book and sing again. Take many liberties with tempo. All sing "Brown Bear, Brown Bear, what do you see?" Only the children with the

brown bear puppets sing the response, "I see a red bird looking at me." Repeat the process with all singing "red bird, red bird, what do you see"? Only the children holding the red birds reply, "I see a yellow duck looking at me." Continue going through all of the characters of the story. All sing the last sentence together… "That's what we see." Encourage the children to move the puppets so the puppets look like they are singing. This activity allows children to hear themselves singing by themselves or in a very small group,

5. Sing the book yet again, but this time the children choose which character in the story they would like to hold. Have the children stand up in the circle and put the puppet on the floor behind them. They are instructed to move carefully to a different spot in the circle so they can choose their own animal character. In other words, the children move but NOT the puppets. You need the puppets in order of the story so the children can look at them to know what to sing. The children will generally no longer need the book!

Chicka Chicka Boom Boom

By Bill Martin. Jr. and John Archambault
Coconut Tree
(alphabet)

1. Read the book *Chicka Chicka Boom Boom* by Bill Martin, Jr. and John Archambault. Sing the song at the appropriate time during the reading. Even when the words have changed slightly, make the song fit to match the words.

2. When the tree gets overloaded with letters and it tips over in the story add egg shakers on the chicka chicka text, a drum on the BOOM BOOM text, and a slide whistle when the alphabet letters all fall off of the tree. Children LOVE to make their own sound effects!

3. The coconut tree in the picture is sort of an interactive tree. You can buy a coconut tree with sticky letters, but this has more action for the children. The tree is made from a sturdy wooden base with felt cut to resemble the tree trunk. A clear plastic bowl container was affixed to the top in order to hold the letters. Plastic palm leaves were glued on. The last step in assembly is to tie some

clear fishing line around the base of the leaves at the top of the tree.

4. Purchase or make coconuts. I couldn't find any so I bought some plastic kiwi fruit from the store. Close enough, I figured!

5. Buy or make alphabet letters (I used all upper case) and paint them. I bought about four of each letter and spray painted each a different color, using only four colors total. Using all of the alphabet letters at once seemed a little overwhelming for my PreK children so I used only eight letters at a time. I passed out one letter A–G to each child, making sure there were maybe three A's, maybe two G's, and all four colors represented in some manner. Each child is holding a letter. Then you start to paraphrase the book. Speak slowly *"A..."* and a child who is holding the letter A must put the letter in the plastic bowl. When you say "told **B**..." holding the letter B will put their letter in, and so on. When you sing "the coconut tree" lyrics, have a child put a coconut (or kiwi) in the tree bowl.

6. I have other adults in the room with me and one of them holds the fishing line. They were instructed to pull the tree down gently when the area was clear of children, so the tree would not fall upon a child. The children scream with delight when the tree falls and contents fall out. Really hype up the excitement about putting the pieces in the tree bowl. Allow the tree to wobble on occasion to add to the anticipation of making the tree fall.

7. Switch letters and coconuts so each child gets to place something different in the tree bowl and play again.

Coconut Tree

Kathy Costanzo

Strega Nona

By Tomie dePaola

Never Touch the Pasta Pot!

Kathy Costanzo

Enough, Enough

Kathy Costanzo

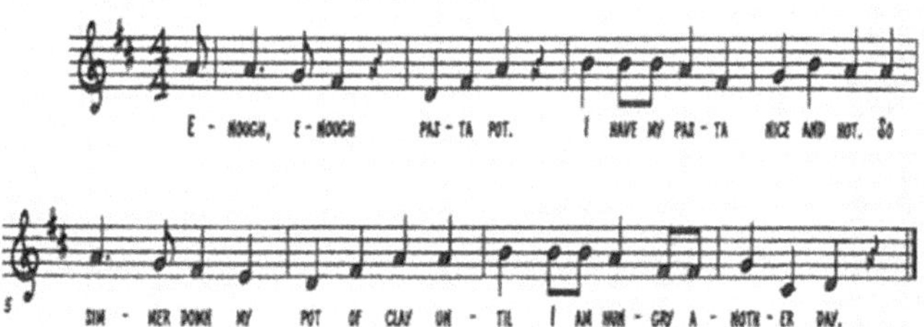

Bubble, Bubble Pasta Pot

Kathy Costanzo

Happy Song

Kathy Costanzo

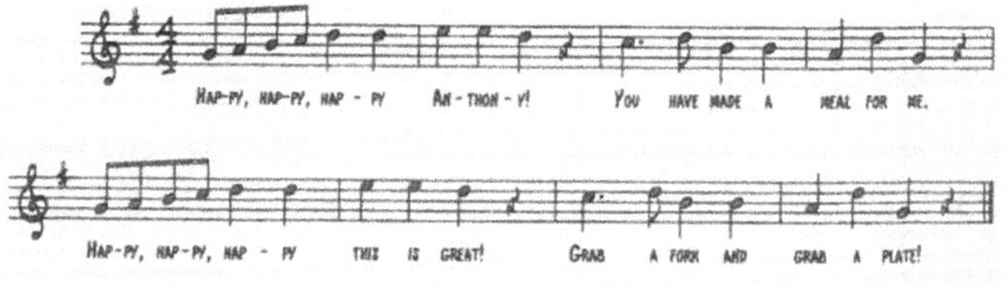

Strega Nona
Song Instructions

Never Touch the Pasta Pot!

Sing, instead of read, this part to the children. The B section is sung in Italian. It translates to "do not touch." You can skip that part if you do not feel comfortable with the Italian.

Bubble Bubble Pasta Pot and Enough, Enough

These are the same songs but with different lyrics. Don't forget the three kisses after Strega Nona sings "Enough, enough!"

Happy Song

Create some lively dance or jig to perform while the children are singing. Make it a "happy dance."

It has been said…
- that in the Italian language, Strega Nona means "Grandma Witch."
- that there are 10 books in the "Strega Nona" series.

The Gingerbread Man

19th-century fairy tale

The Gingerbread Man

Kathy Costanzo

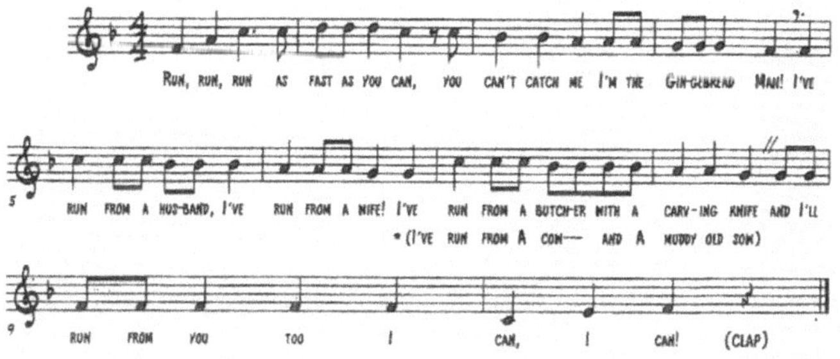

Spoken: NO! NO, I won't come back! I'D RATHER RUN THAN BE YOUR SNACK!

COME BACK! (Jazz hands up every time you say this)

It has been said…

- the gingerbread house became popular in 19th century Germany after "Hansel and Gretel" was written by the Brothers Grimm.

- that English Queen Elizabeth I is credited for the first gingerbread men. Previously, European monks created gingerbread in the shape of angels and saints.

- that National Gingerbread Days are on June 5th and November 21st.

The Gingerbread Man
(dramatization)

1. Read the book aloud to the children. When the text reads "Run, run, run…" sing that section instead of simply reading it. As more characters are added to the story, sing more lyrics accordingly.
2. Use a rhythmic, sing-song type of talking voice for the "No! No! I won't…" section of the story.
3. Use jazz hands as a show of excitement for the "Come back!" section.
4. Print a color picture of the Gingerbread Man and laminate the picture. You will need at least six more pictures than the number of children you are teaching.
5. Cut the head off at the mouth of the Gingerbread Man.
6. Glue the top of the head separately from the bottom on a hinged clothespin, Use the kind that you pinch open and closed. This will look like the Gingerbread Man is opening his mouth to sing or talk.
7. For any section that is spoken/sung by the Gingerbread Man, use the clothespin paper puppets for acting out the story.

You need more puppets than children because someone always decapitates their Gingerbread Man. Simply trade out a broken one for a whole one,

The Very Hungry Caterpillar

By Eric Carle

Munch

Kathy Costanzo

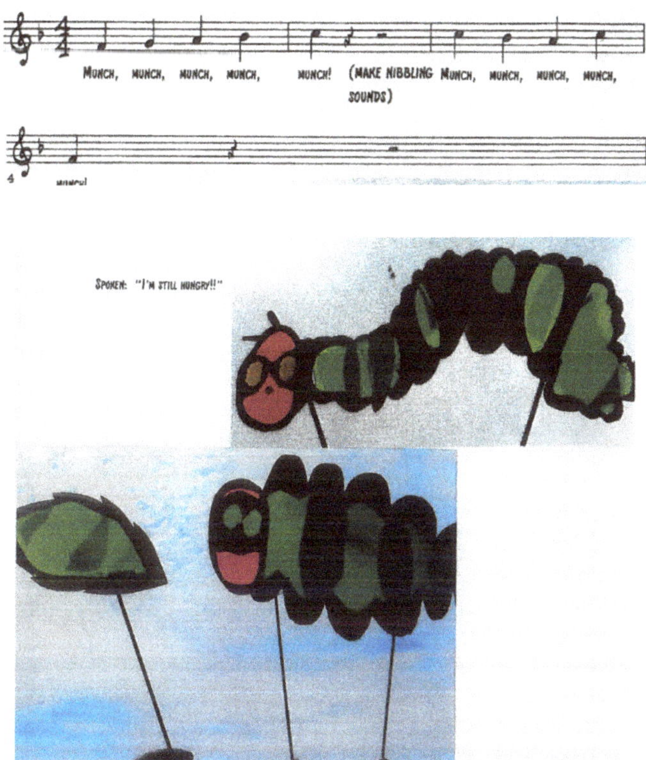

Munch
(dramatization)

1. I love to dramatize this story! I bought a Very Hungry Caterpillar stuffed animal, poked holes in the bottom of two sides, and added dowels that I glued in place. If you move the dowels together and apart gently it appears that the caterpillar is moving.

2. Make color copies of the food that is eaten during this Story, then laminate the pieces. Use everything to retell and dramatize the story, really make it come to life!

3. Put some costume butterfly wings on a child and allow him/her to pop out at the end of the story.

4. Our puppet club made shadow puppets of the story's characters and food. We put fasteners in the caterpillar, the effect is to make the caterpillar look jointed, and used two skewers in order to make the caterpillar look like it was moving. I also purchased various colors of cellophane. We glued the colors to the back of the puppets and added skewers to all of the foods as well. Sometimes we doubled the cellophane in some places to give the food the same color effect that Eric Carle does by overlapping his colors. When you have a light behind the puppets to project onto a thin white screen the colors show through the puppets and really have a nice effect! Shadow puppets are a lost art.

www.ingramcontent.com/pod-product-compliance
Lightning Source LLC
Chambersburg PA
CBHW042101150726

48005CB00033B/1546